Fairy and Fantasy 4
Grayscale Coloring Book
by Christine Karron

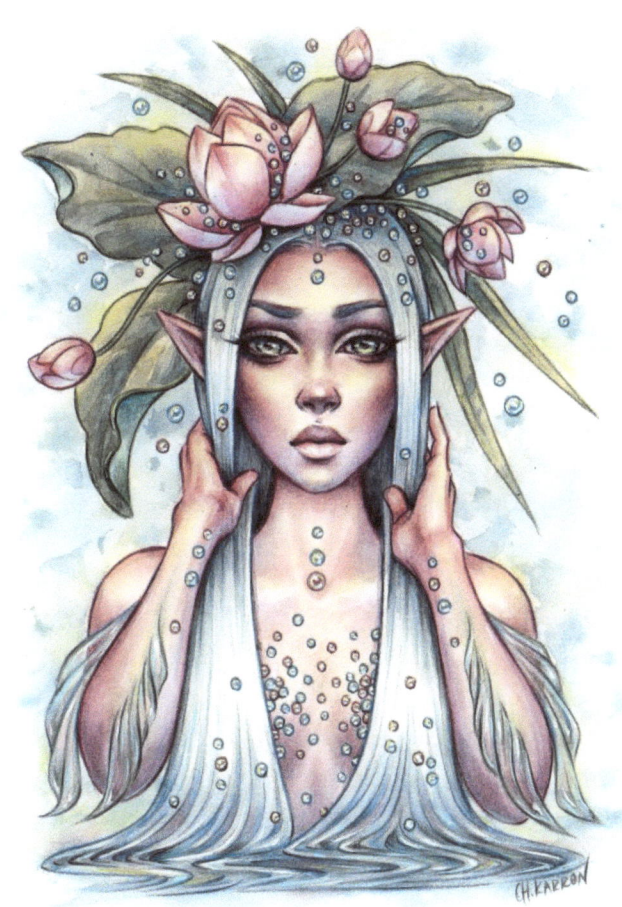

All illustrations in this book were originally created and traditionally hand drawn by the artist Christine Karron. For coloring inspirations, videos and more about Christine's artwork visit www.chkarron.com

This coloring book is suitable for all ages and skill levels. Recommended for coloring with markers, colored pencils, pens and crayons. If using wet media, place a sheet of thick paper or card stock behind the coloring page to prevent bleed through.

FAIRY and FANTASY 4
Grayscale Coloring book by Christine Karron

First published March 2023

Copyright © 2023 Christine Karron
All rights reserved.

Other than for personal use or book review, no part of this book may be reproduced or transmitted in any way, in whole or part without written permission from the copyright holder.

ISBN: 9798387424601
Imprint: Independently published

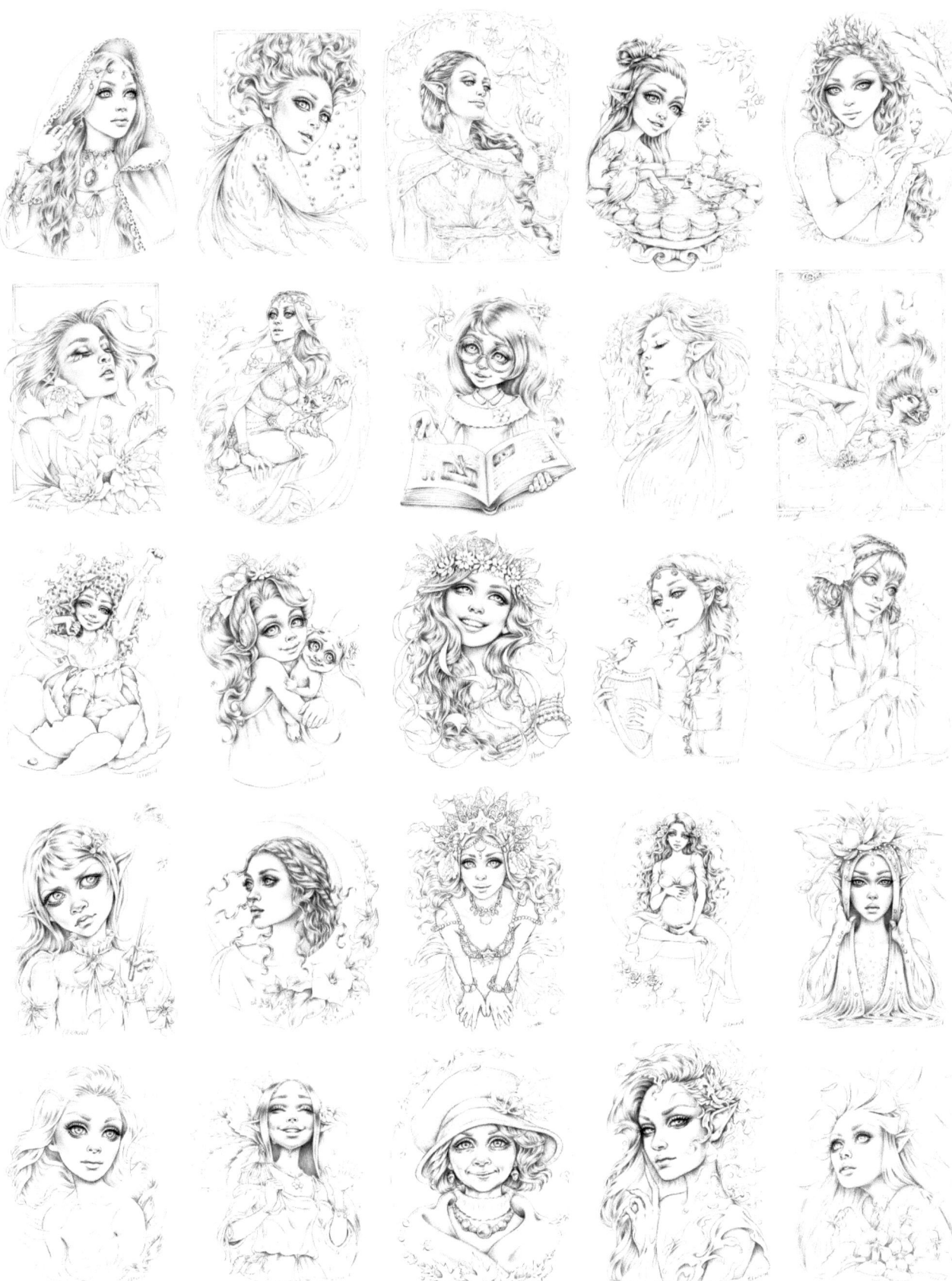

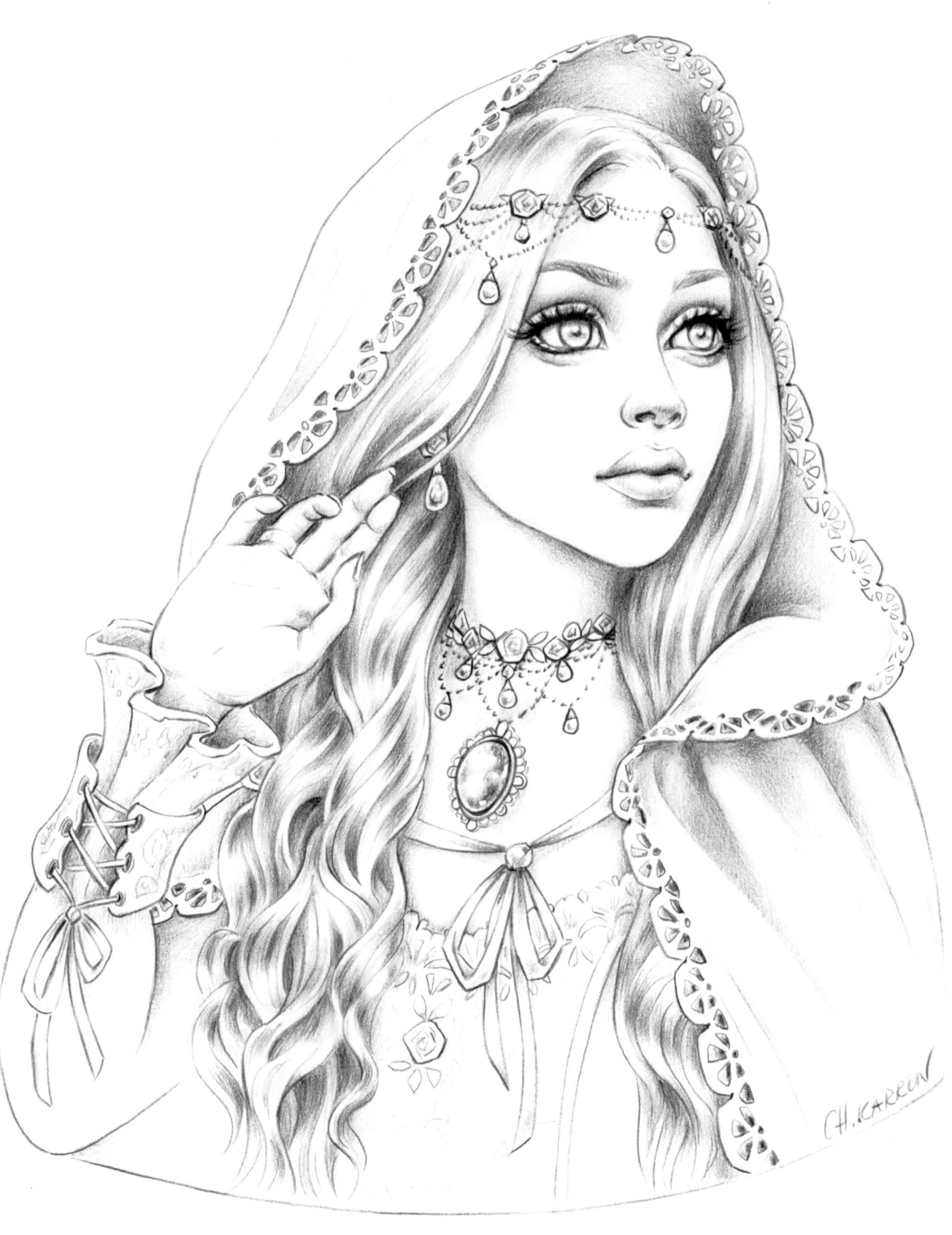

Fairy and Fantasy 4 — Amber

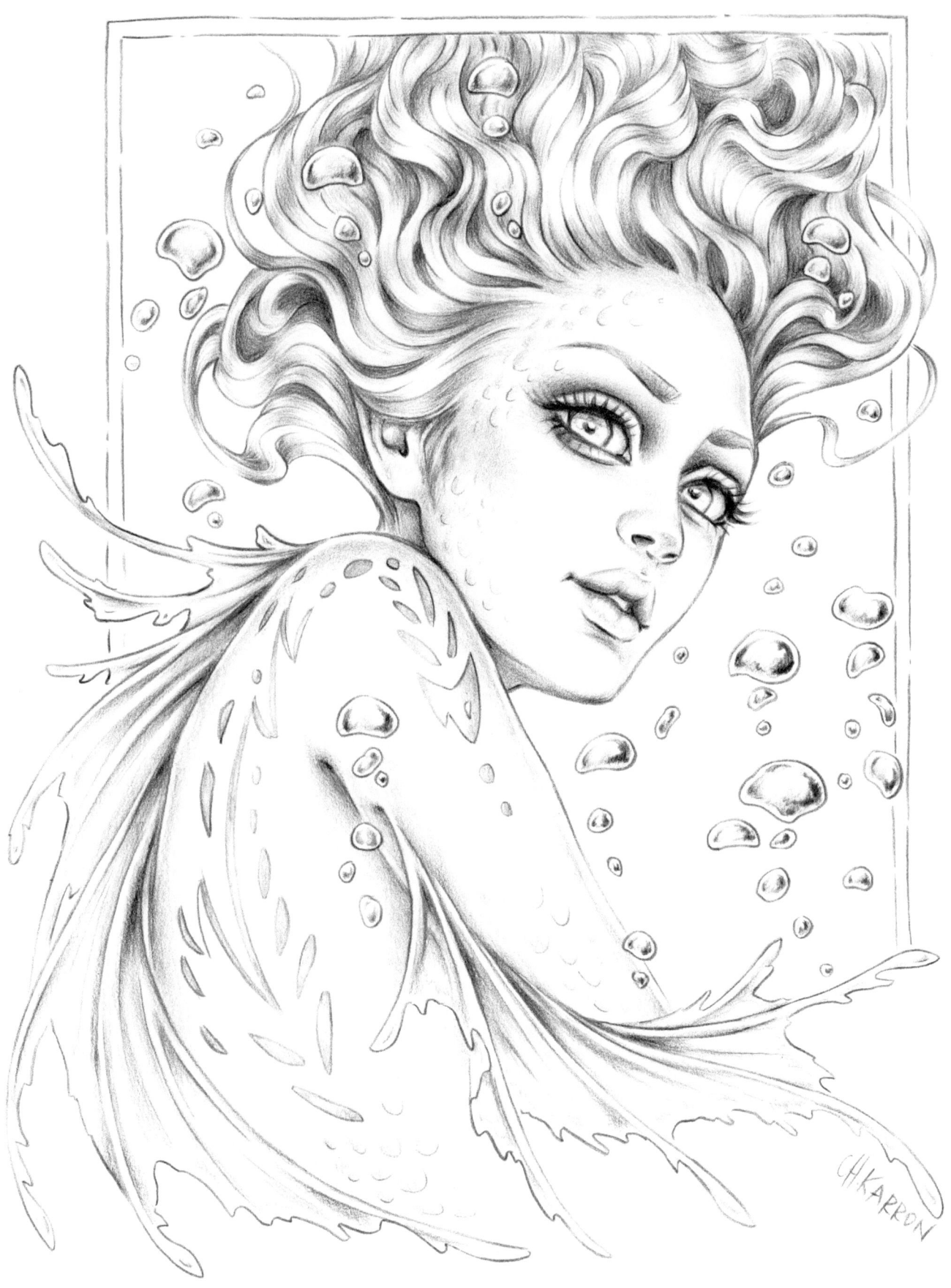

Fairy and Fantasy 4 — Aqua

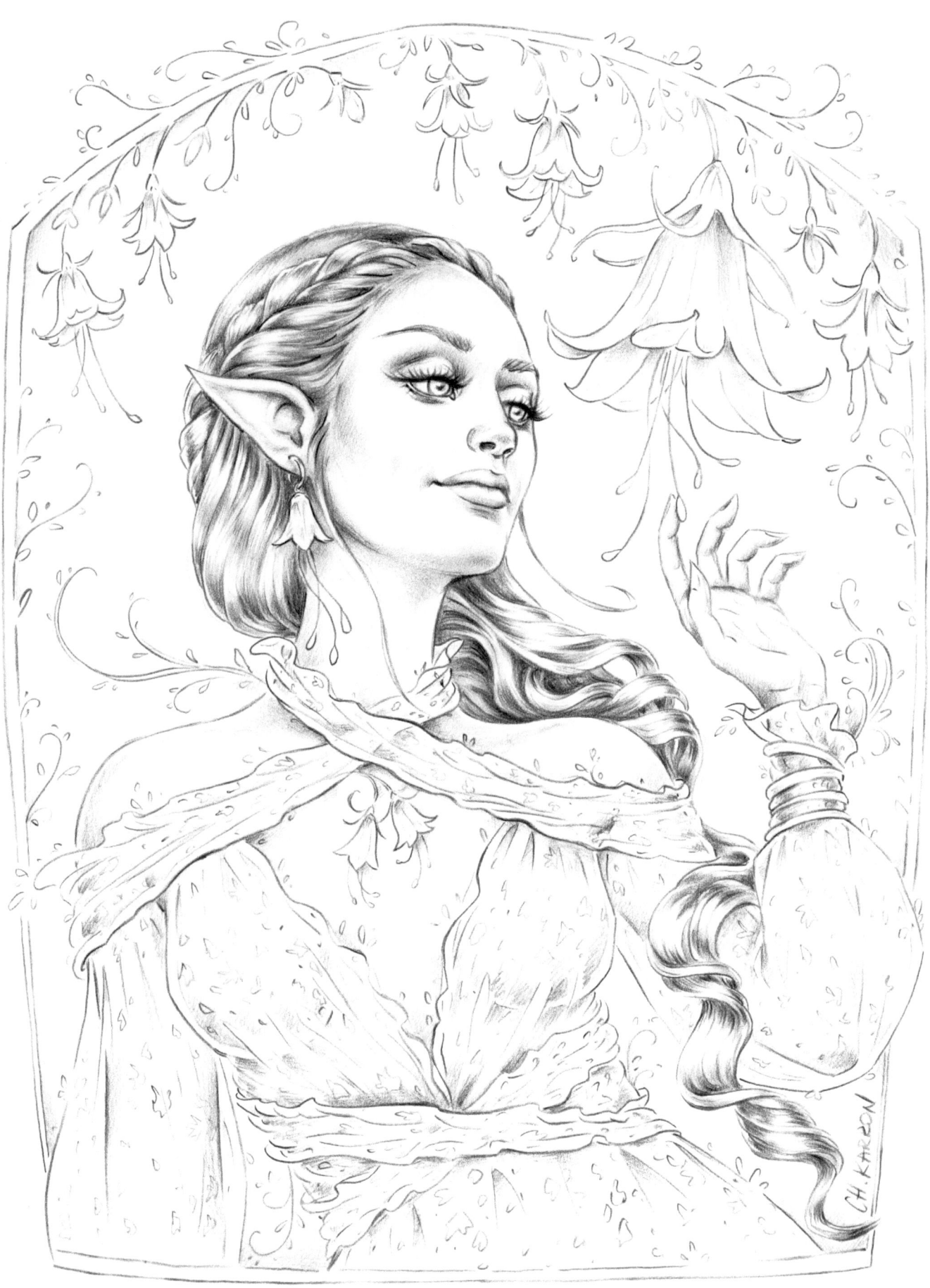

Fairy and Fantasy 4 — Bells

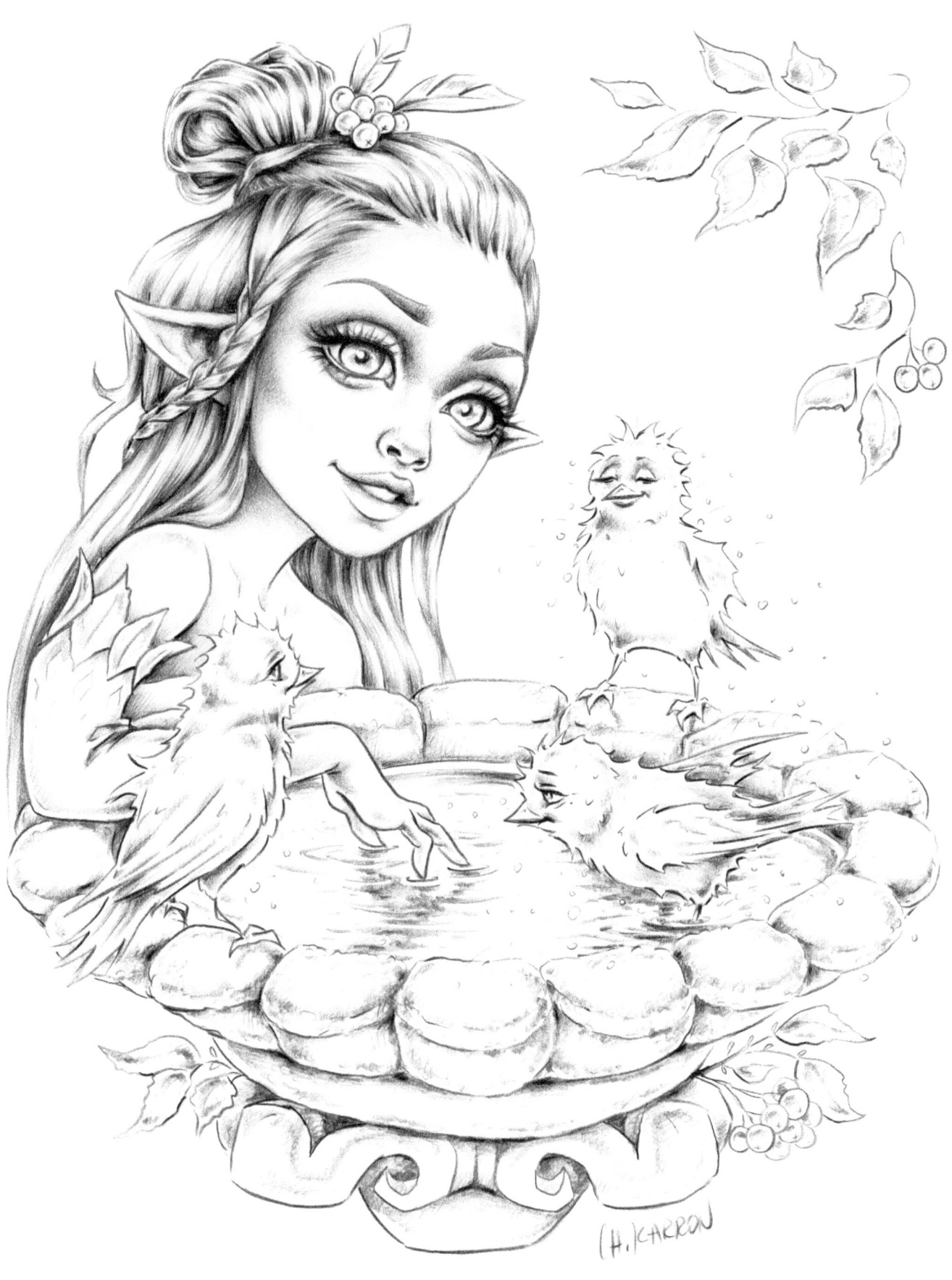

Fairy and Fantasy 4 — Bird Bath

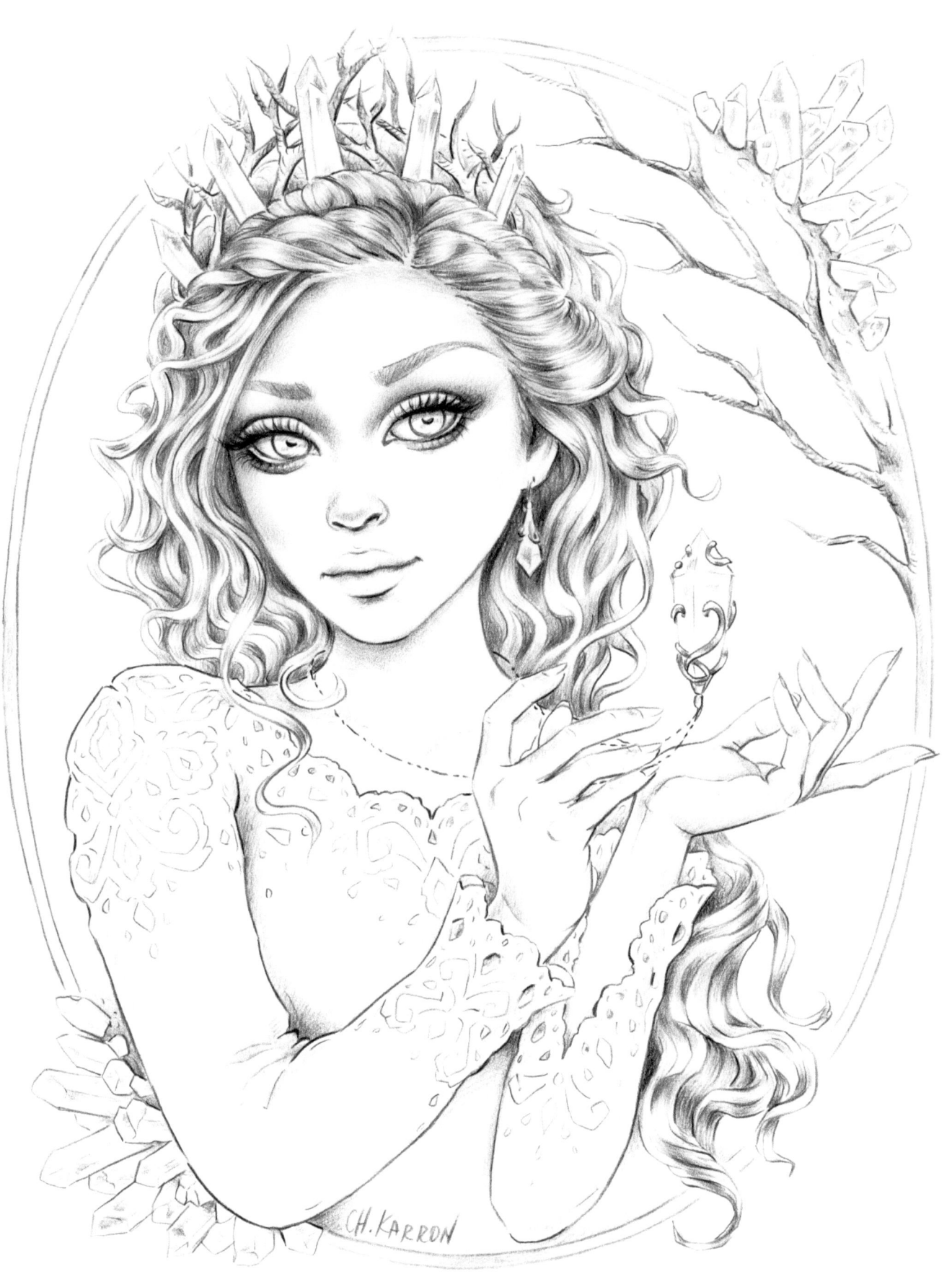

Fairy and Fantasy 4 — Crystal

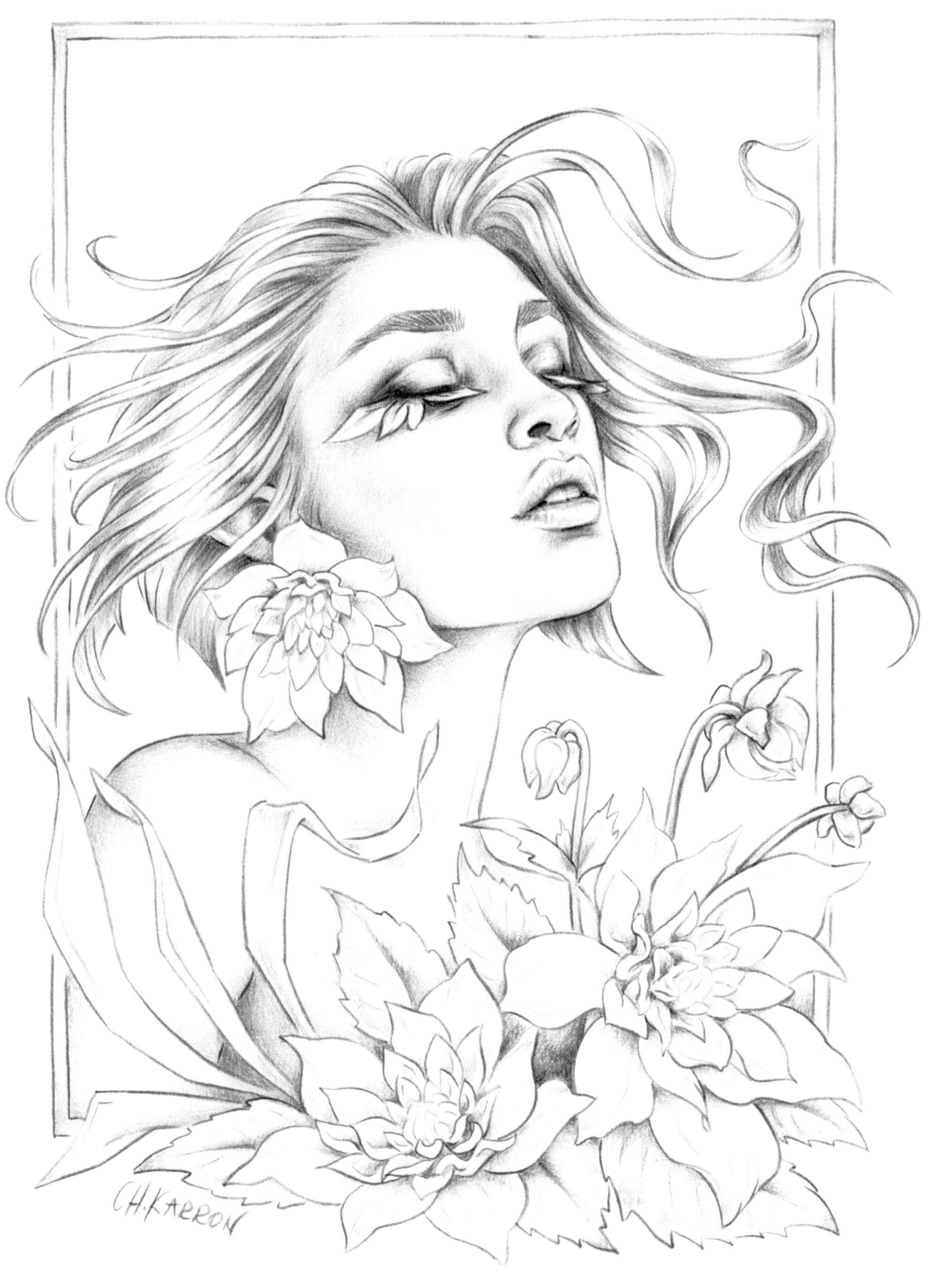

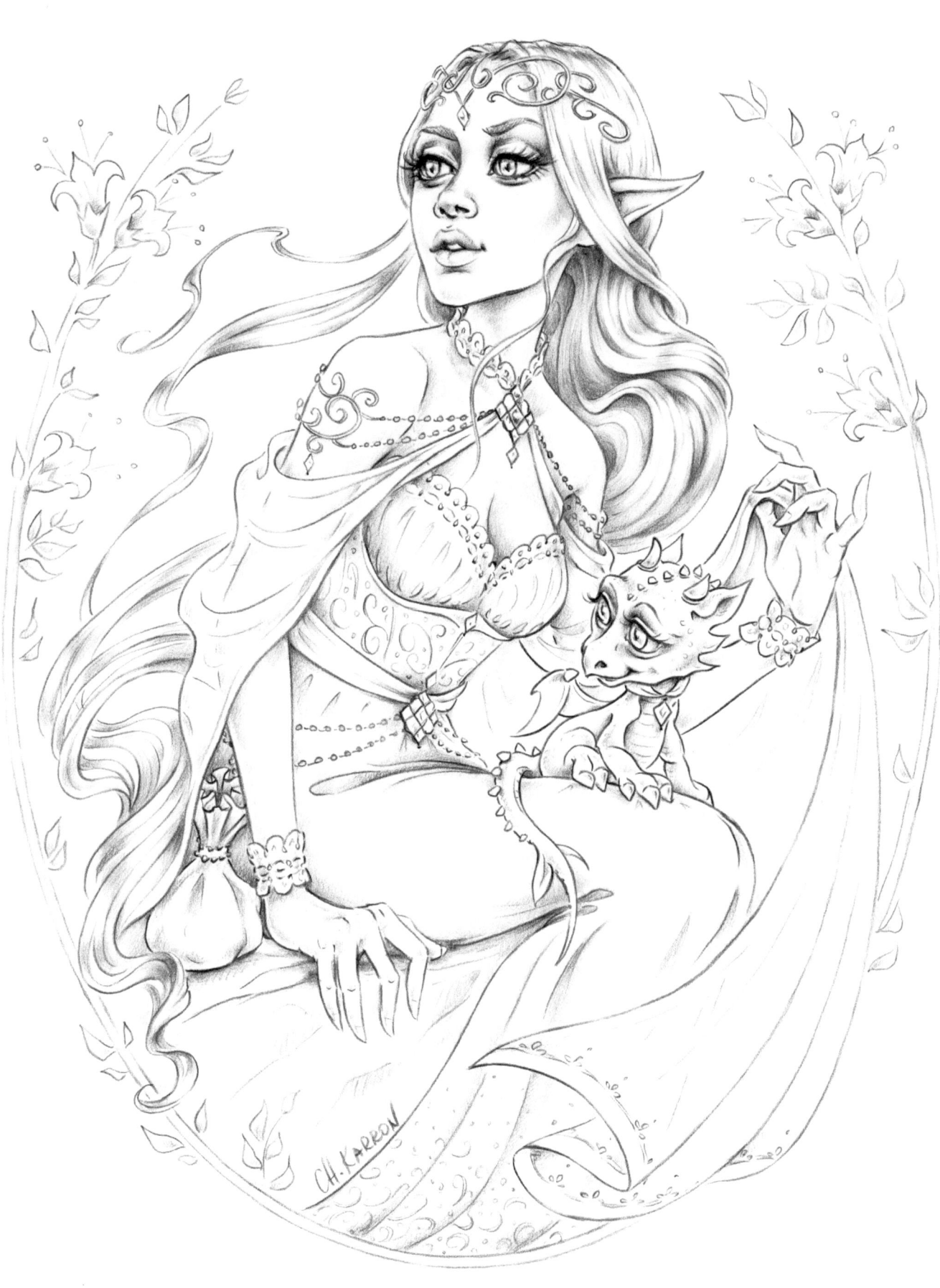

Fairy and Fantasy 4 — Dragonling

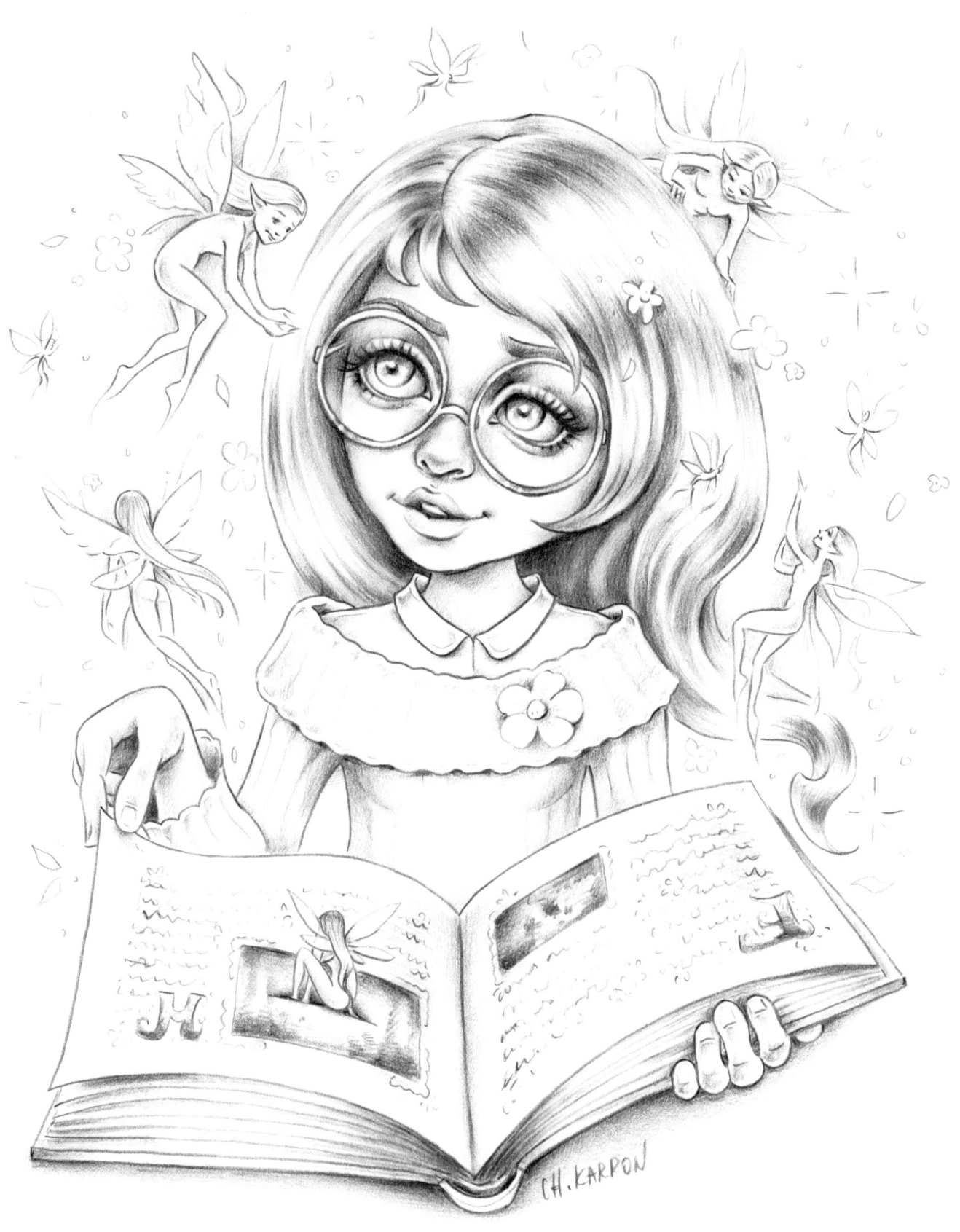

Fairy and Fantasy 4 — Fairy Book

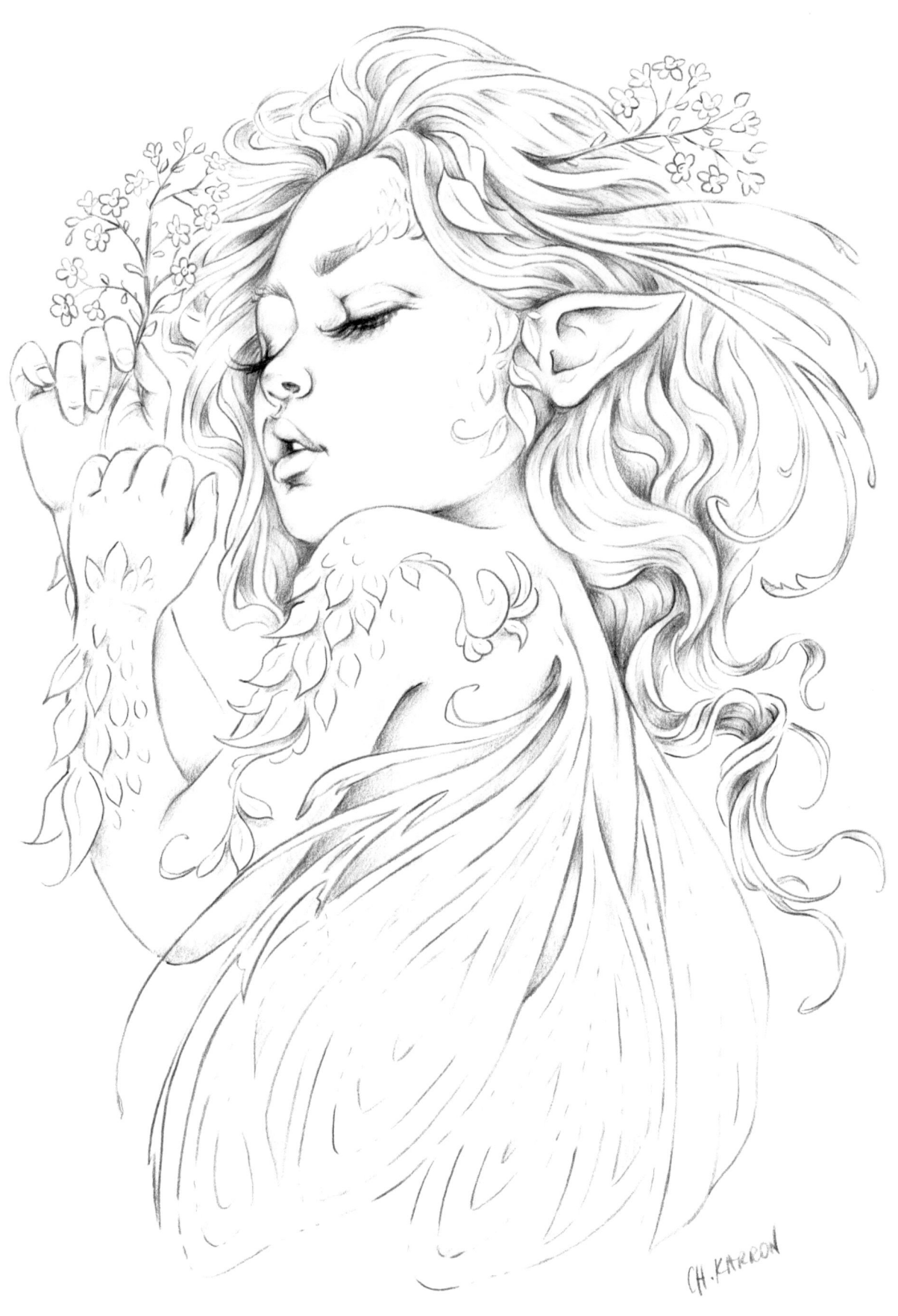

Fairy and Fantasy 4 — Faye

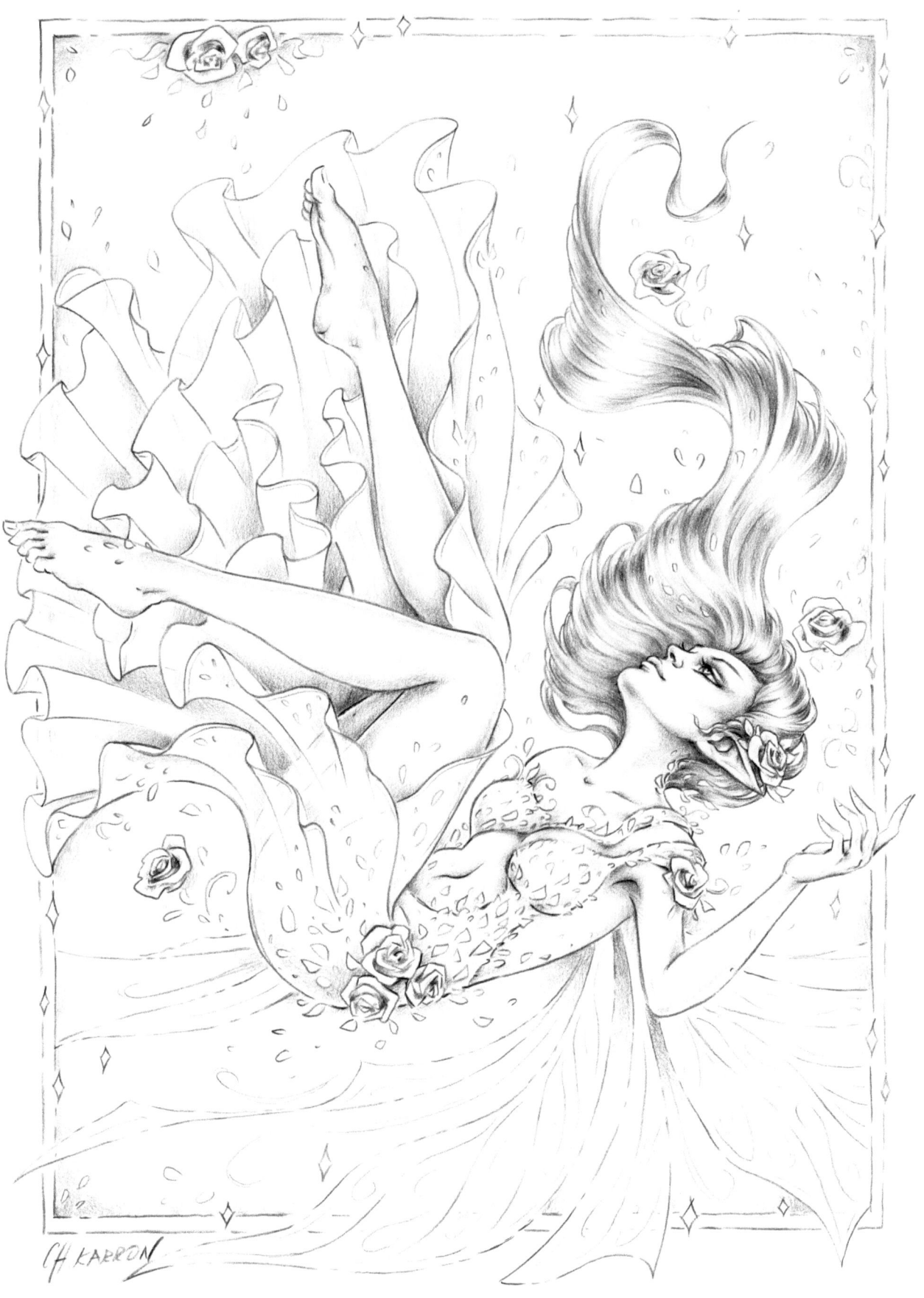

Fairy and Fantasy 4 — Free Falling

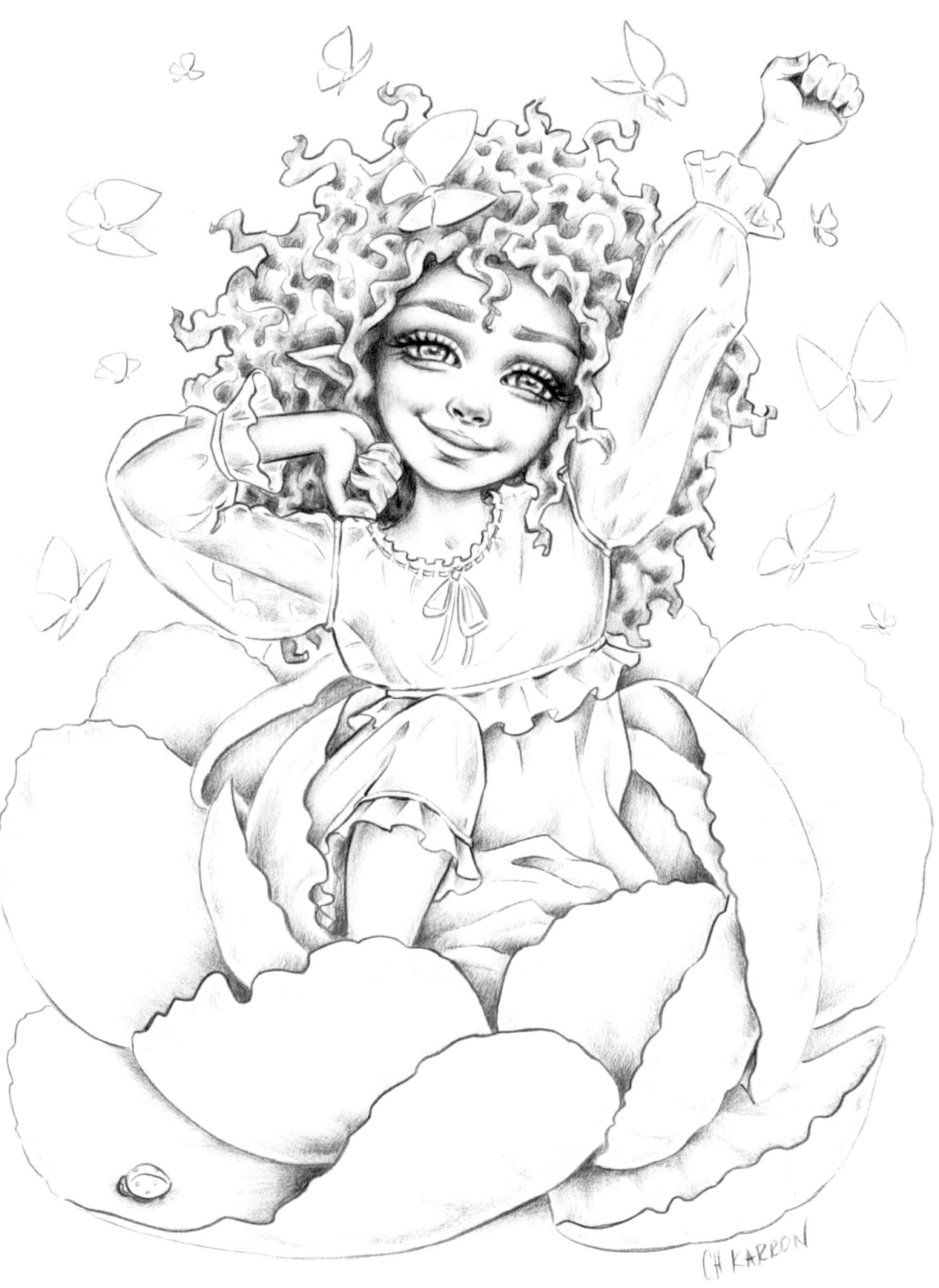

Fairy and Fantasy 4 — Good Morning Fairy

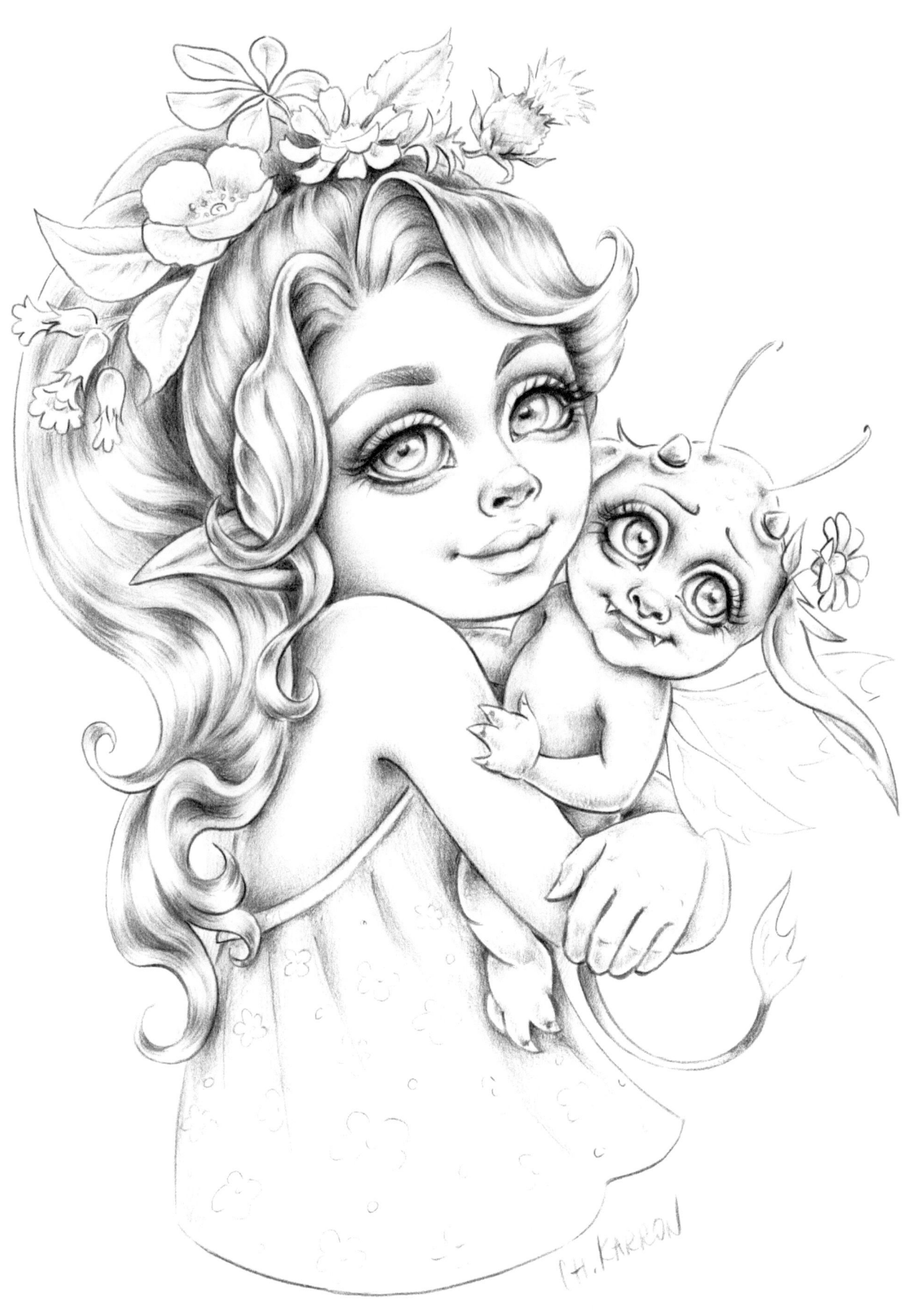

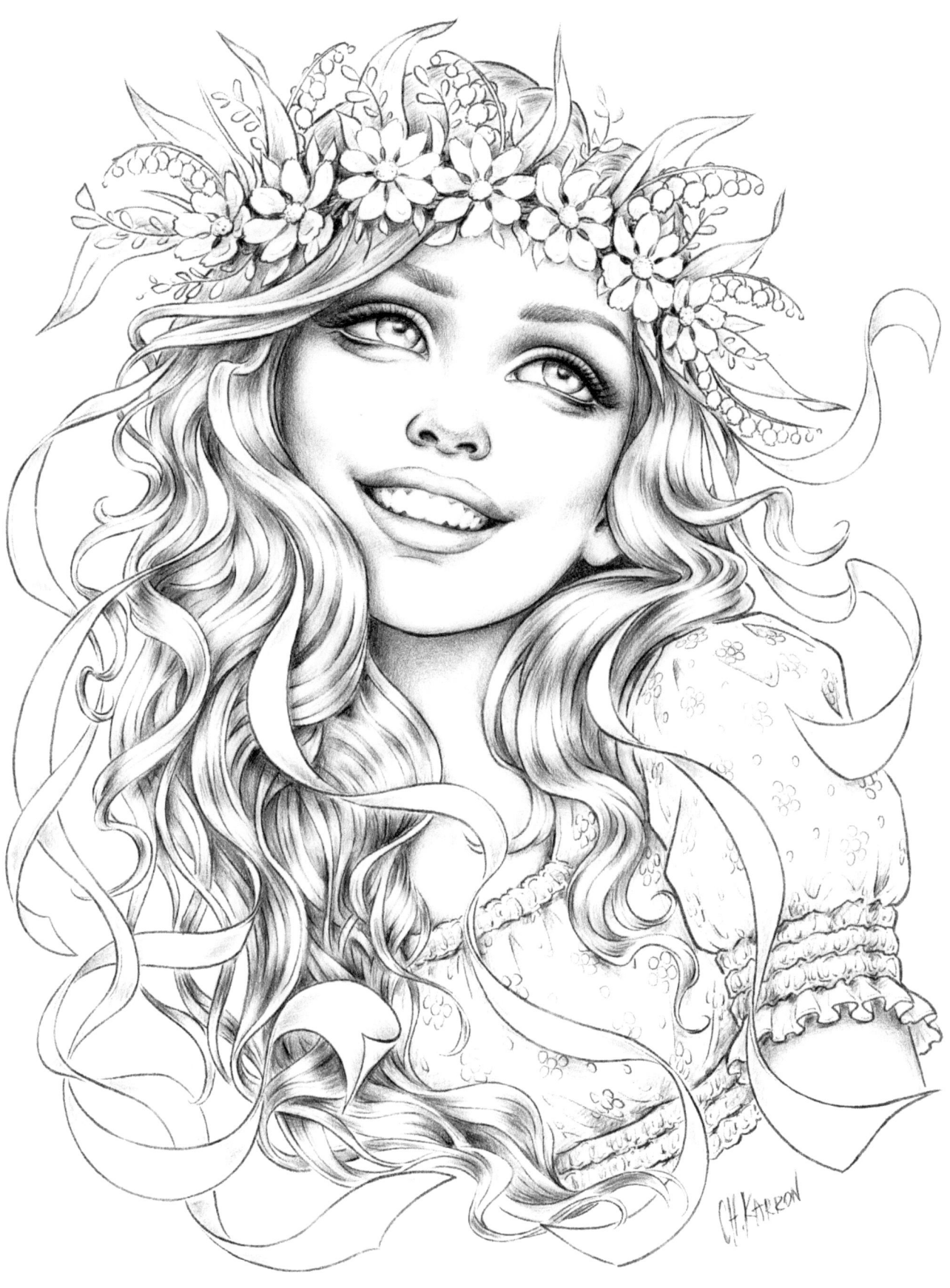

Fairy and Fantasy 4　　　　　　　　　　　Mae

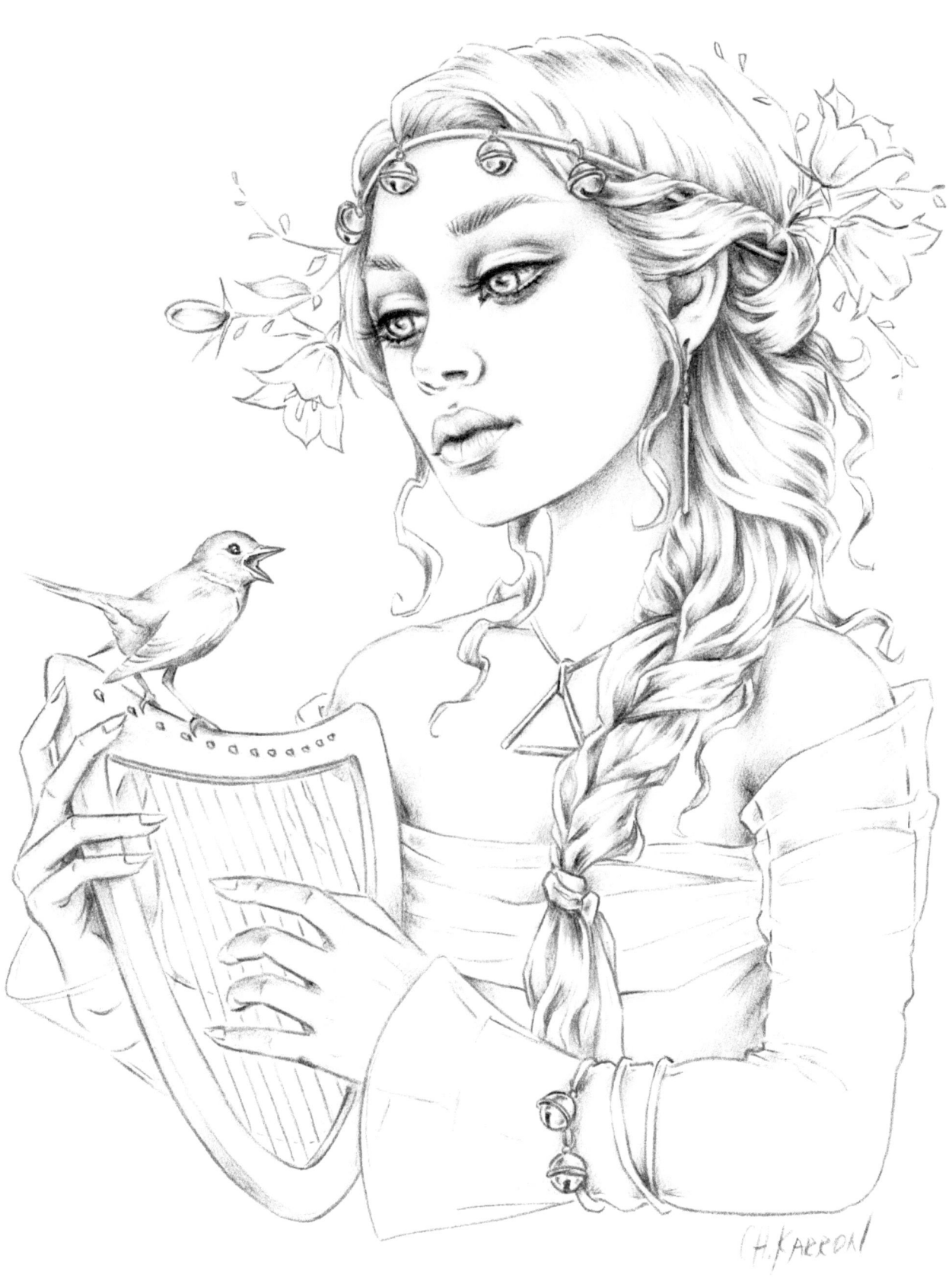

Fairy and Fantasy 4 — Melody

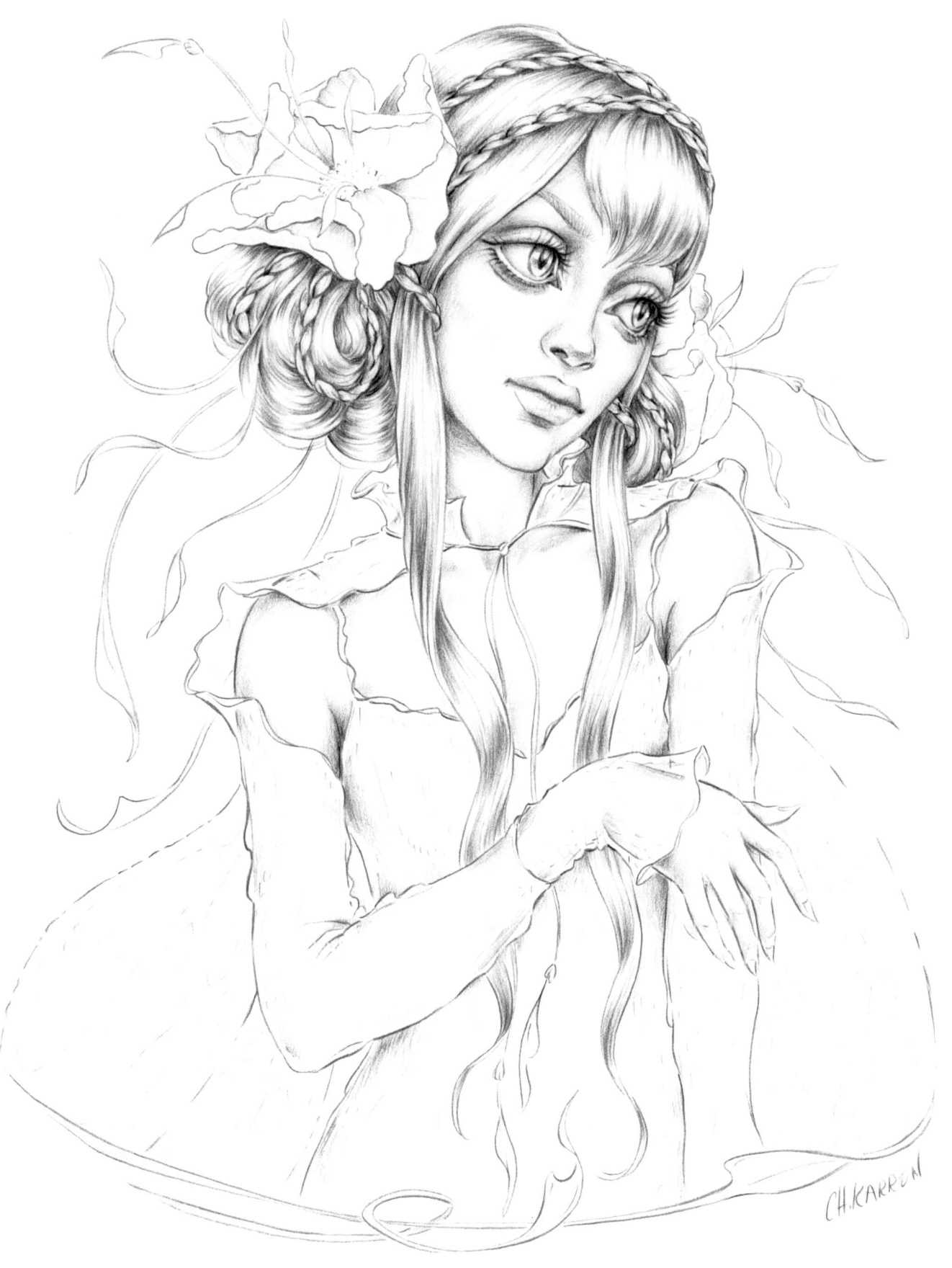

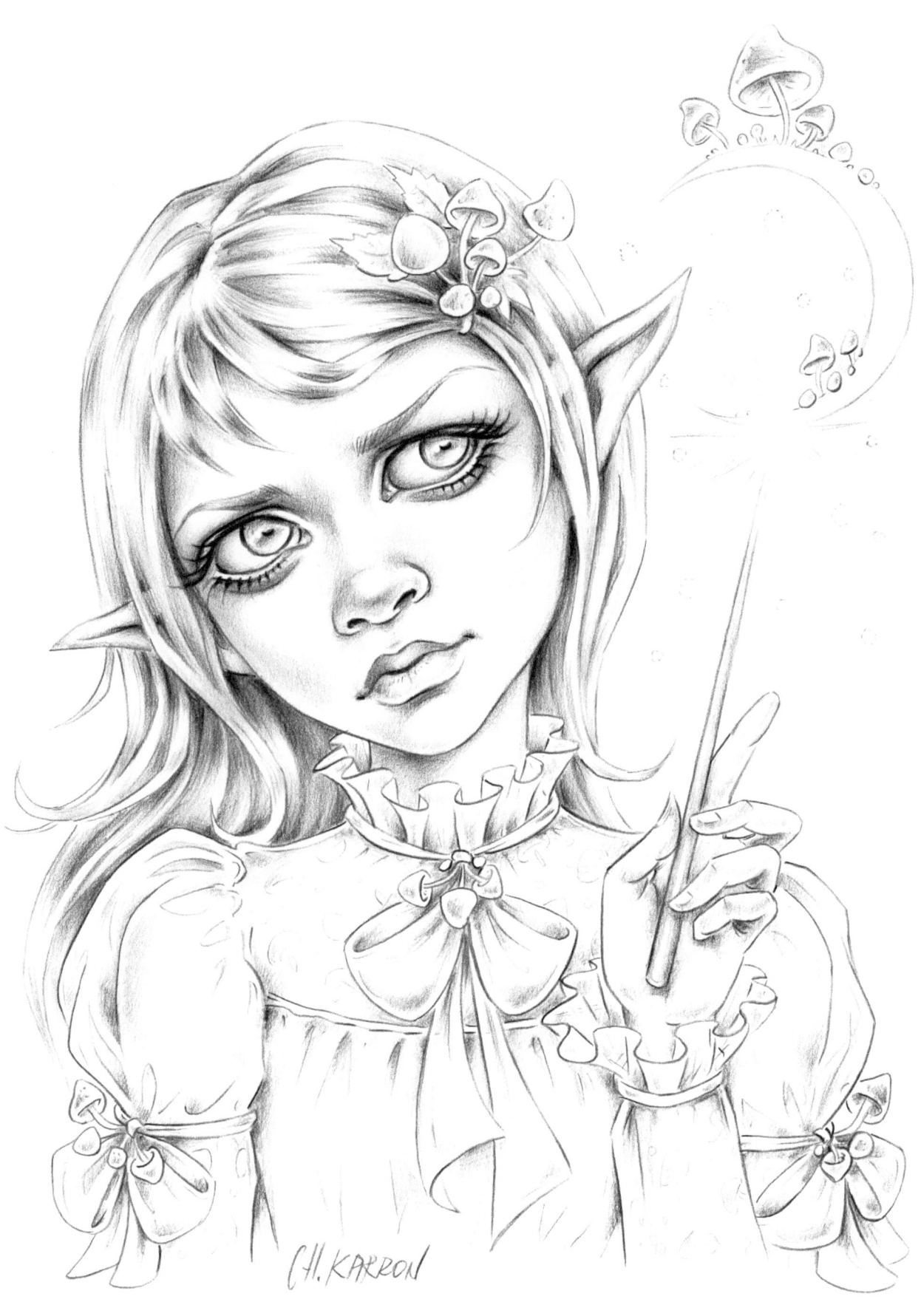

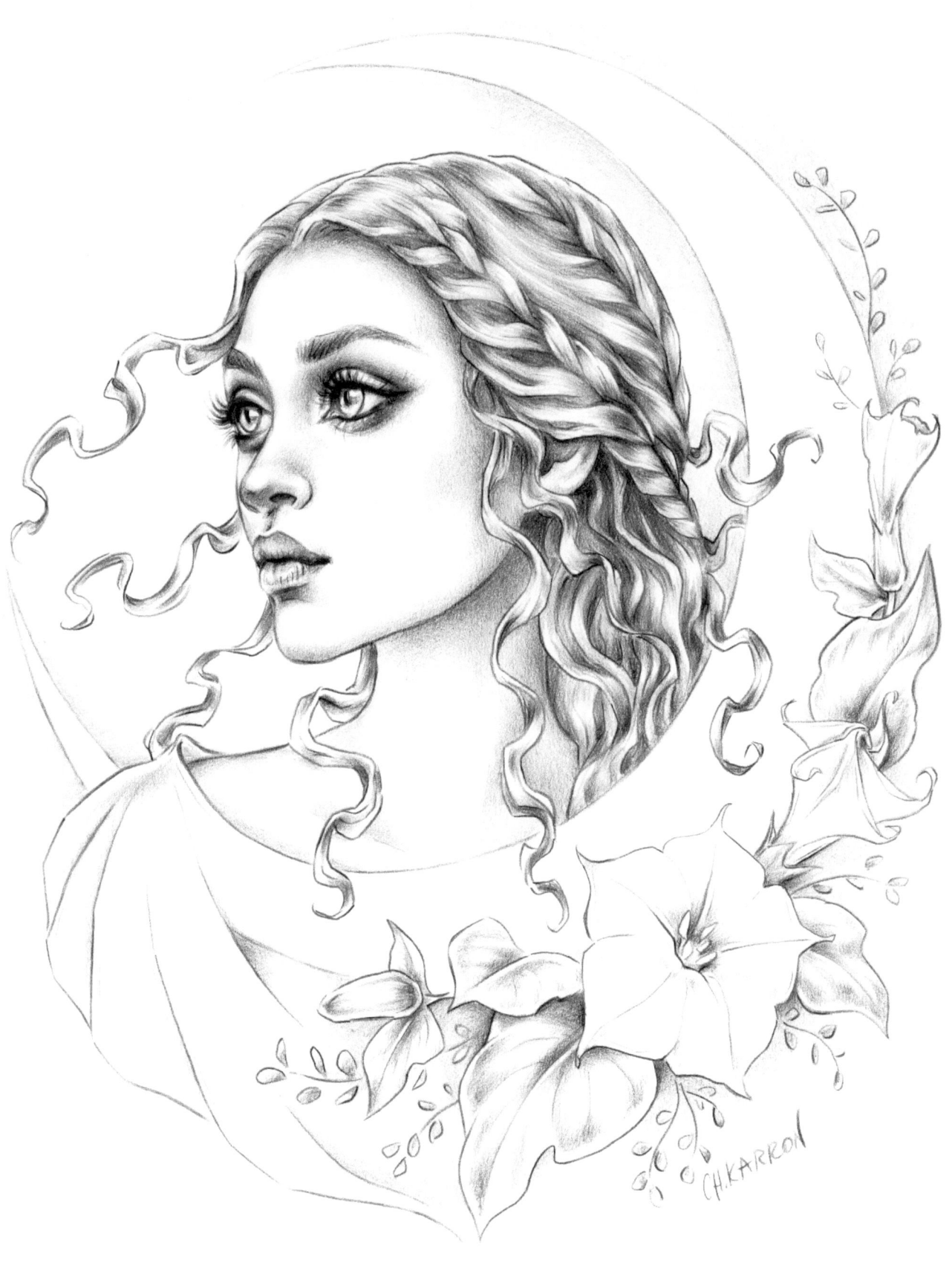

Fairy and Fantasy 4 — Neoma

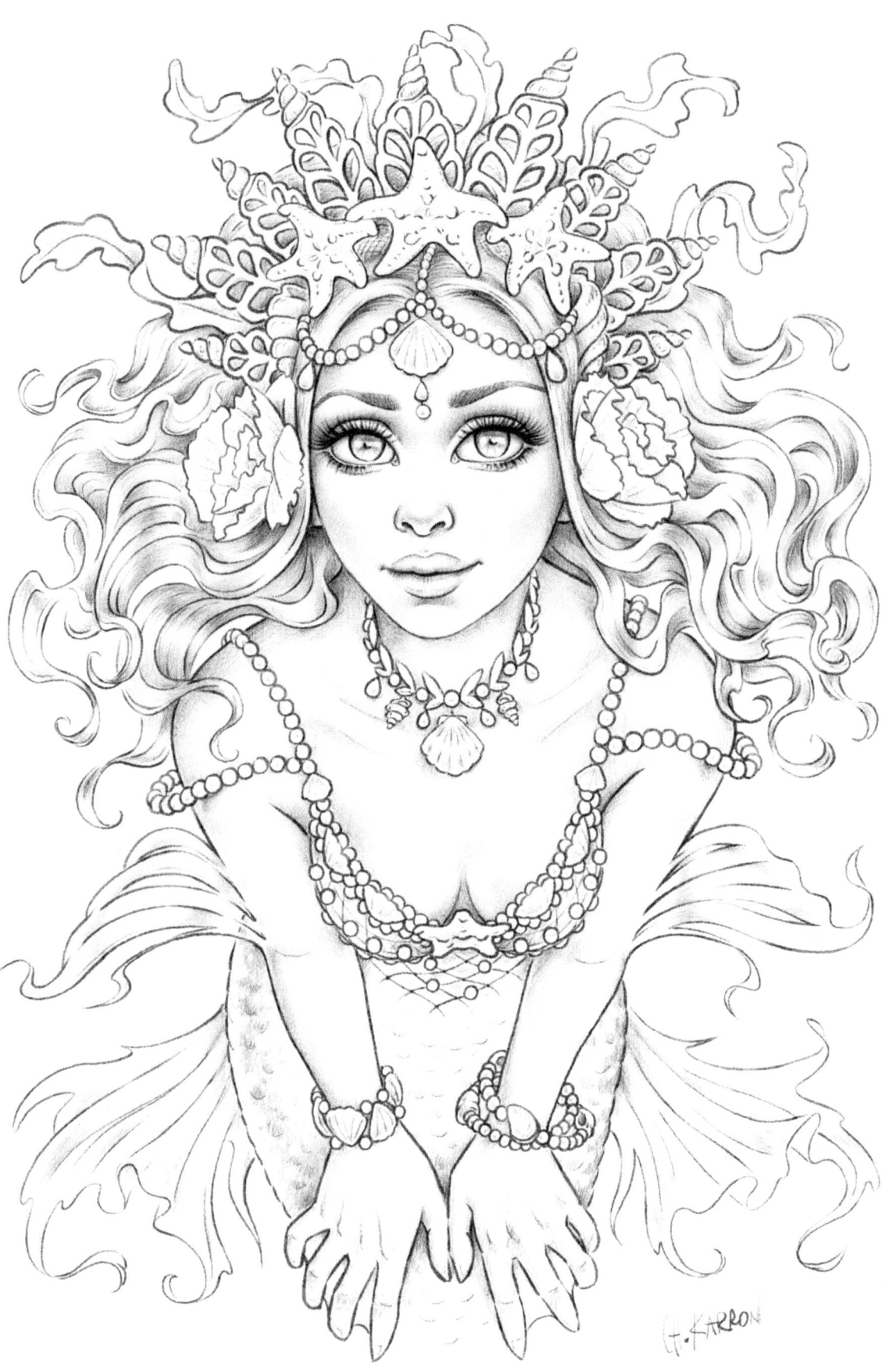

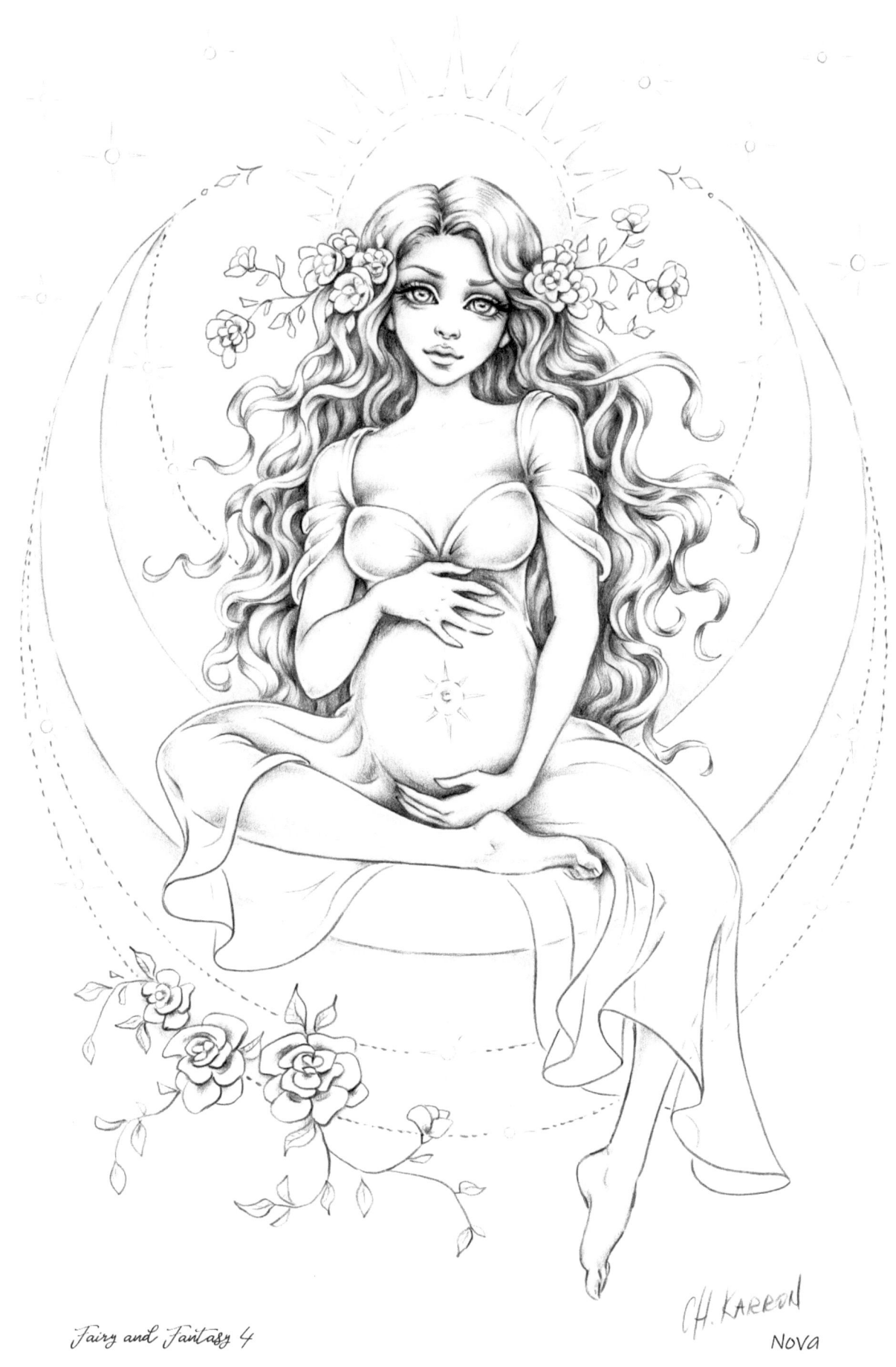

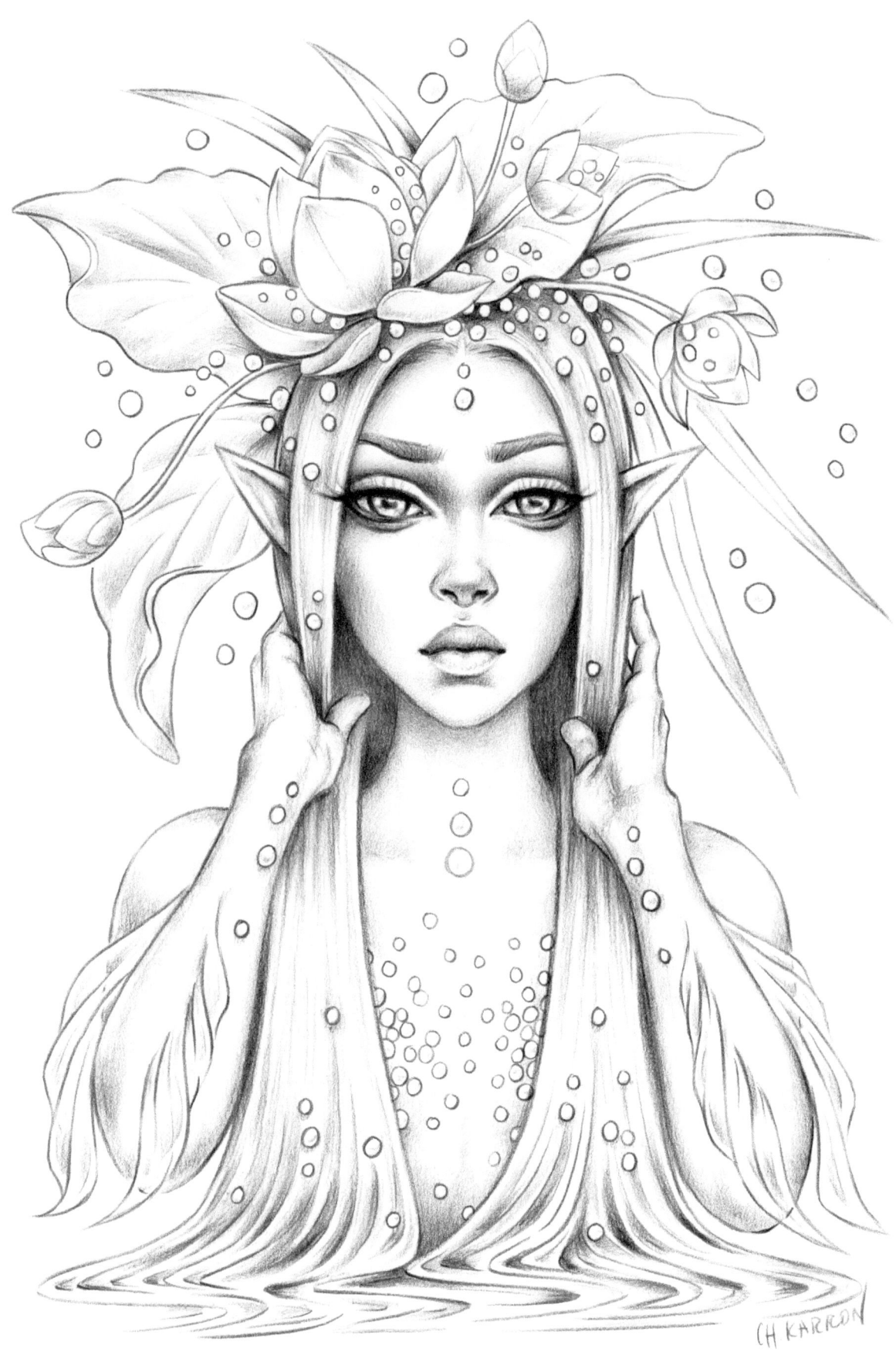

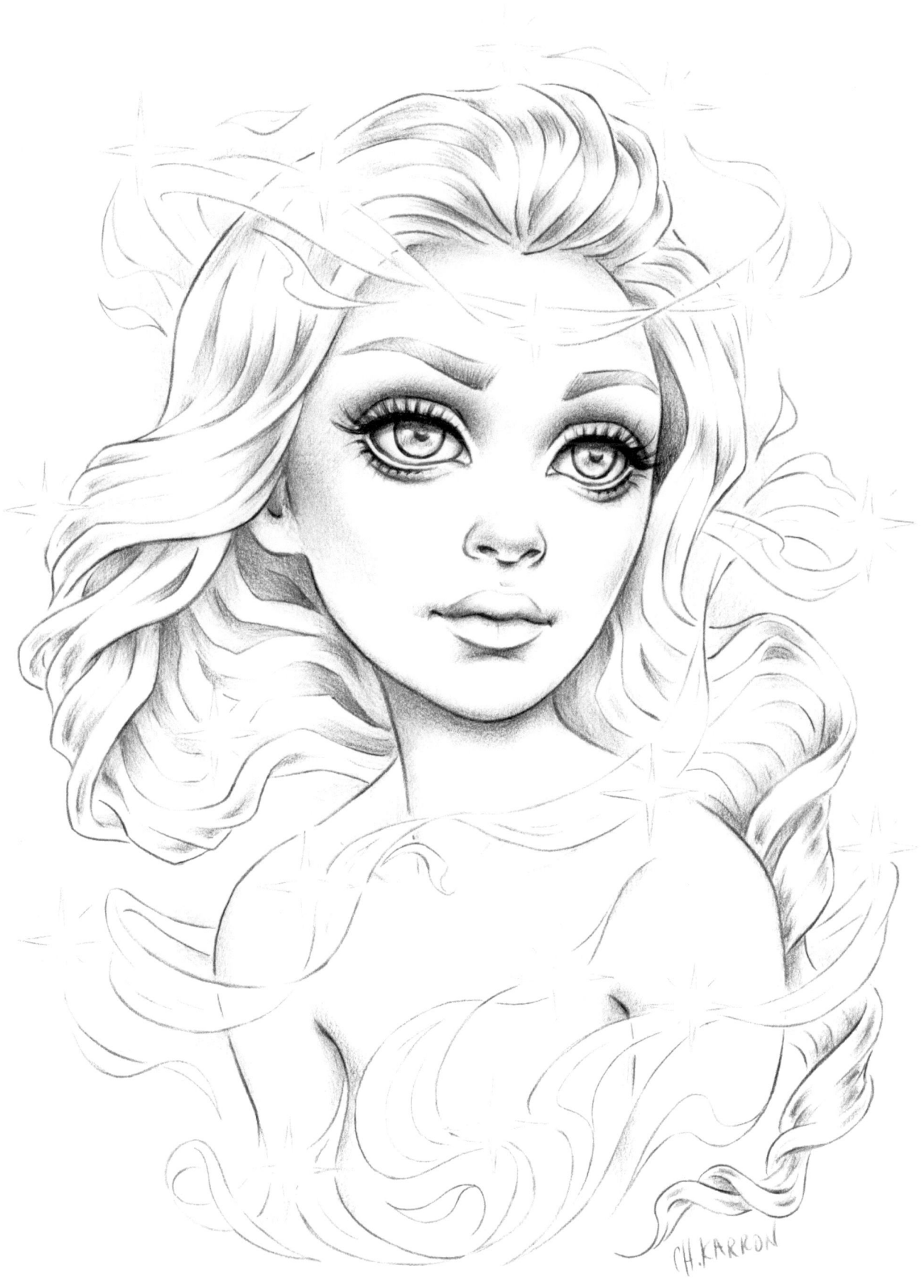

Fairy and Fantasy 4 — Stella

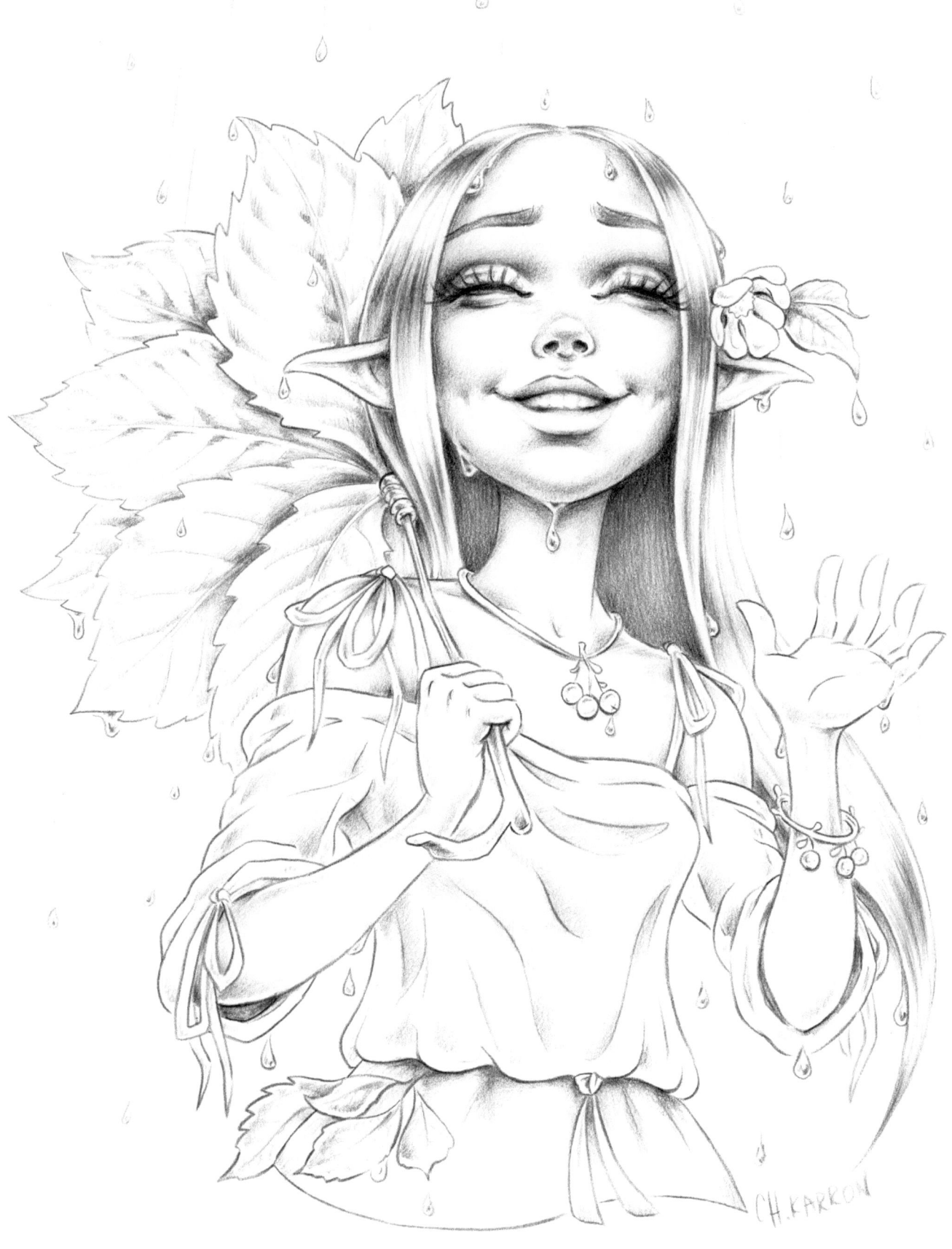

Fairy and Fantasy 4 — Summer Rain

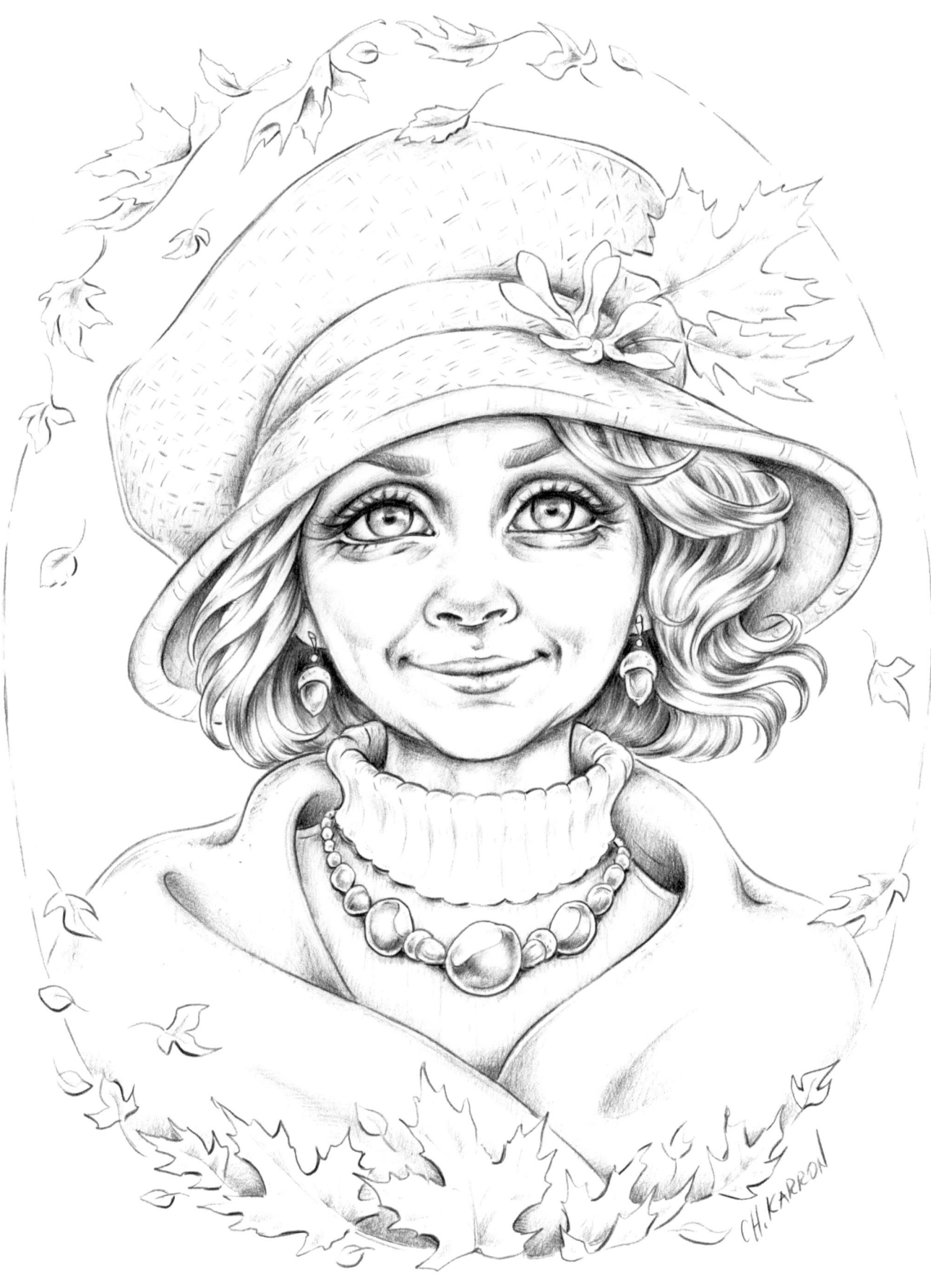

Fairy and Fantasy 4 — Sweet Maple

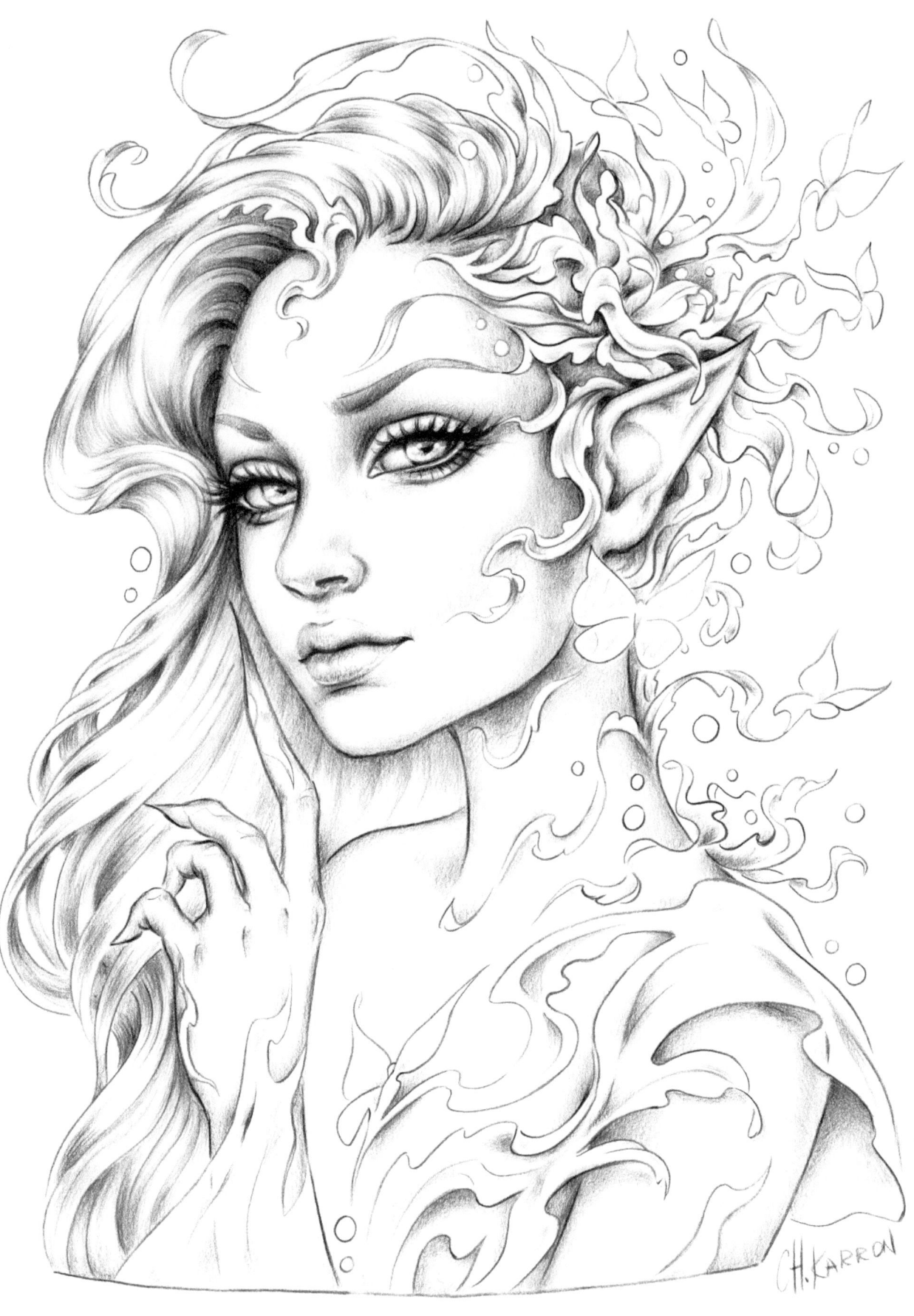

Fairy and Fantasy 4 — Tranquil Grace

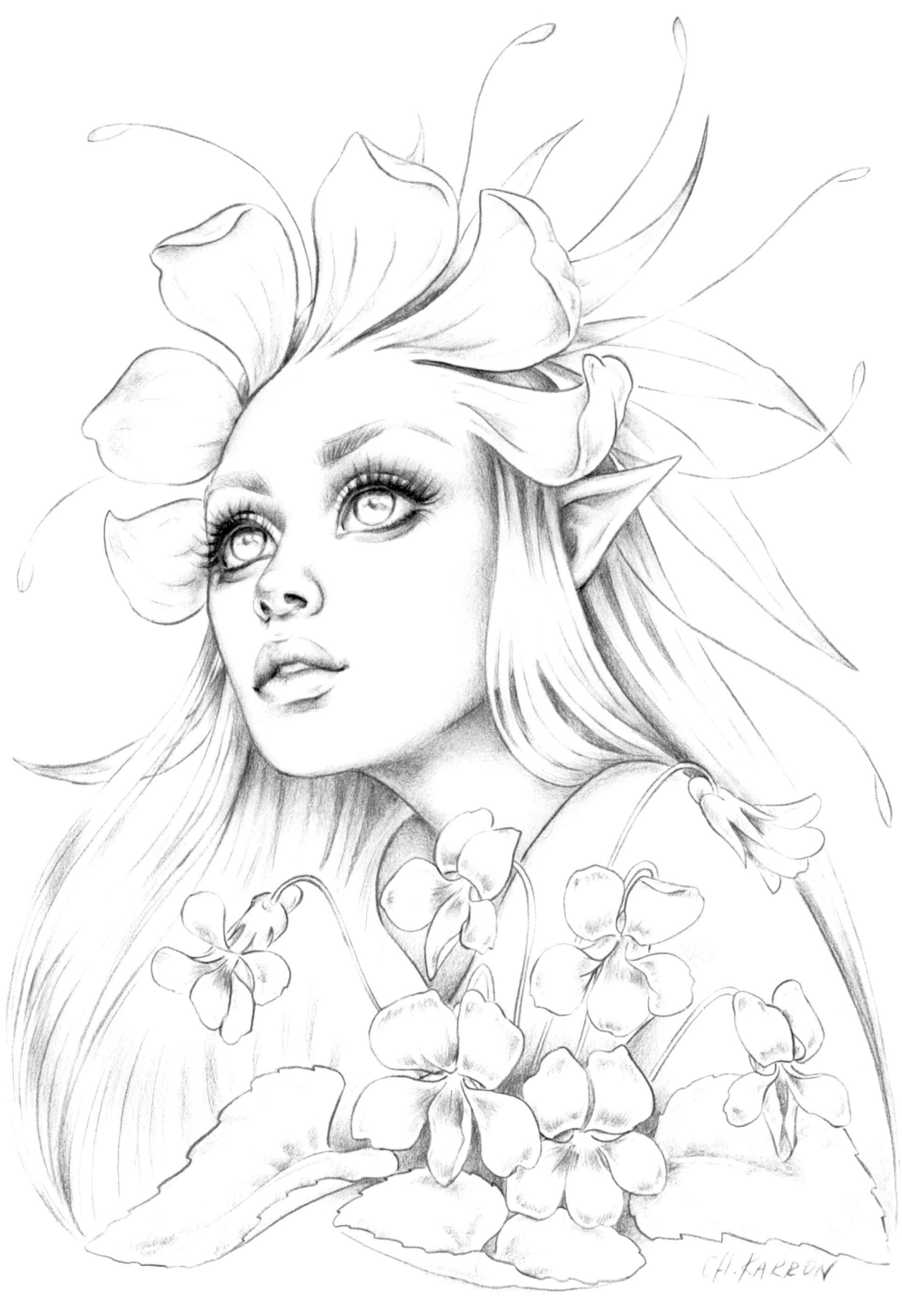

Fairy and Fantasy 4 — Viola

Also available:

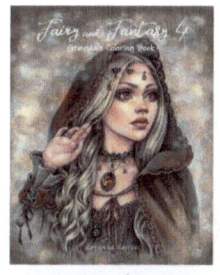 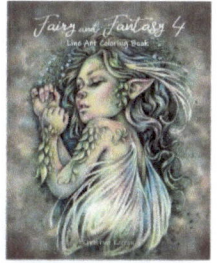 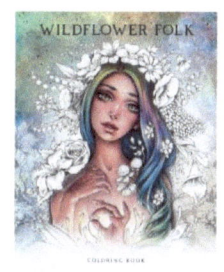 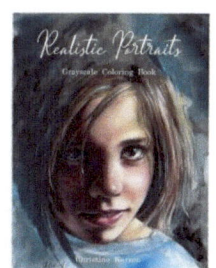
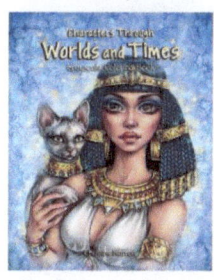 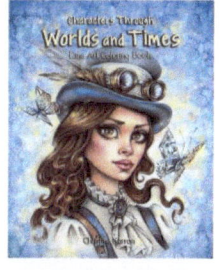 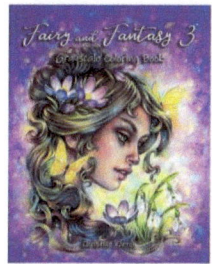 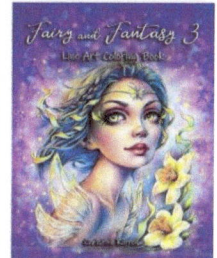
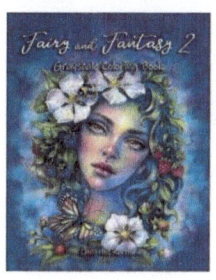 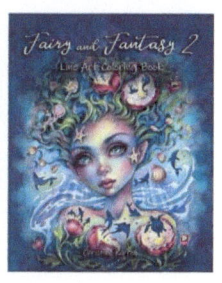 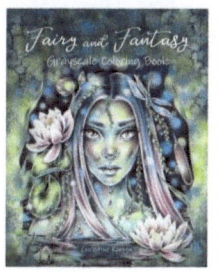 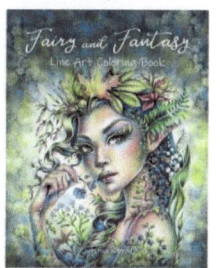
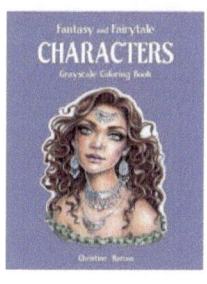 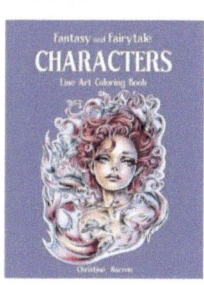 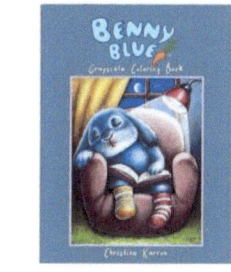 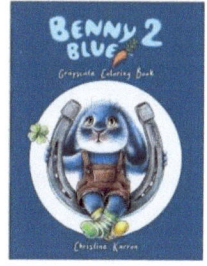
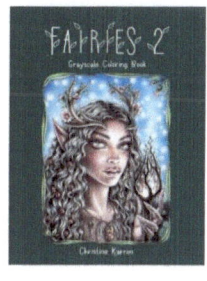 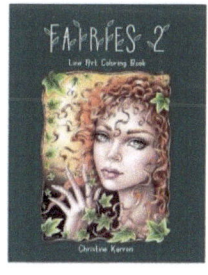 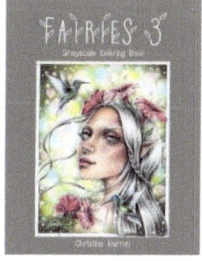 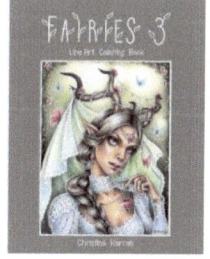
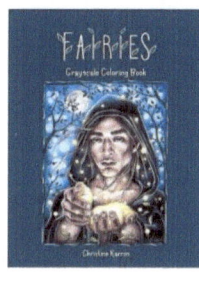 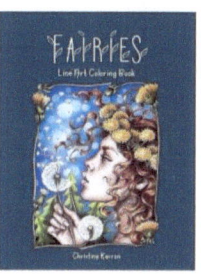 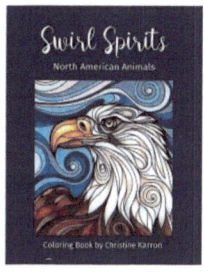 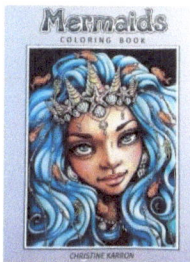

Printable digital coloring page downloads on Etsy:
https://www.etsy.com/shop/ChristineKarron

YouTube videos:
https://www.youtube.com/@chkarron

Instagram: @chkarron
https://www.instagram.com/chkarron

Christine Karron Art and illustration
https://www.facebook.com/chkarron

Christine Karron Coloring Collection Fan Group
https://www.facebook.com/groups/ChristineKarronCCFG

#christinekarron
#chkarron

www.chkarron.com

www.ingramcontent.com/pod-product-compliance
Lightning Source LLC
Chambersburg PA
CBHW051214220526
45473CB00003B/1028